Simple Money Moves For Young Adults

*How to Build Wealth Early,
Spend Smarter, and Stay out of Debt*

By
Gerardo Avila

Publication Date

Aug 29, 2025

Language

English

ISBN

9798993285405

Category

Education & Language

Copyright

All Rights Reserved - Standard Copyright License

Contributors

By (author): Gerardo Avila

Prologue: If I Could Go Back

Most people grow up completely in the dark about money.

We're taught how to drive, pass tests, maybe land a job - but not how to budget, invest, use credit, or build long - term wealth. By the time most people figure it out, it's because they've made a painful mistake.

This book is what I wish I had back then.

If I could go back, these are the lessons I would give to my younger self.
No fluff. No complicated charts. No fake hype. Just simple, real - world advice that would've saved me time, money, and stress.

You don't need to be rich to learn about money.
You don't need a finance degree. And you definitely don't need to wait until it's too late.

Today, information is everywhere. If you've got a smartphone and internet access, you already have more tools than anyone did 20 or 30 years ago. But most people use them for the wrong things - scrolling social media, chasing distractions, staying stuck.

Don't do that.

If you really want to grow, you have to apply yourself. Read. Listen to audiobooks. Watch YouTube tutorials, use ChatGPT, or simply just, Ask questions. There's no excuse anymore - only choices.

One of the biggest traps people fall into is playing the victim - believing that financial freedom is only for the rich, lucky, or connected. I know this because I've been there too. I used to think the system was against me, but that mindset didn't get me anywhere. What I learned is this: the difference between those who grow and those who don't usually comes down to effort, consistency, and a willingness to learn.

The bottom line is who's willing to do the work?

This book is here to get you started. It won't solve every problem. But it'll give you the foundation I wish I had when I was just getting started.

Keep it simple.
Keep it growing.
And don't wait for permission.

Your future self is counting on you.

– Gerardo Avila

Intentionally left blank

Table of Contents

Intentionally left blank

Disclaimer

I am not a financial advisor or a certified public accountant (CPA). The information in this book is based on my personal experiences and the lessons I have learned throughout my adult life. It is intended for educational purposes only and should not be considered professional financial advice. Everyone's situation is different - please consult a qualified financial advisor, CPA, or other professional before making financial decisions.

Introduction

If I Could Go Back

When I was around 20 years old, I bought a brand - new truck. She was a beauty, not to mention very expensive. At the time, it felt like the right move. My dad gave me advice I didn't fully understand.

He said, ***"Son, buy a house first. Then use the equity to buy your truck."***

What he meant was simple: an asset can pay for a liability. A house can grow in value and even give you equity you can borrow against in the future. A truck, on the other hand, only goes down in value. If I had listened, I could have let an appreciating asset buy me the truck, instead of putting myself into more debt.

But I didn't listen. I used the excuse of being tired of having cars that broke down often.

I wasn't thinking about long - term value.
I wasn't thinking about opportunity cost.
I wasn't thinking about how the money I spent on that truck could've been working for me.

I just didn't know what I didn't know.

That's why I wrote this book - because if I could go back, I would've wanted someone to hand me a simple guide like this.

Not a lecture. Not a 400 - page textbook.
Just the truth - clear, real, and easy to understand.

You don't have to be rich to start building wealth.
You don't need to make all the right moves.
You just need to start with a few good ones.

This book will help you:

- Make smarter choices with the money you already have
- Avoid common traps most people fall into
- Build habits that actually lead to freedom

Whether you're earning a little or a lot, just getting started or trying to reset - this book is for you.

Let's keep it simple.
Let's keep it real.
And let's get started.

Chapter 1: Why Money Feels Complicated (But Isn't)

You Don't Need a Finance Degree - You Just Need to Start Early

---

The Waiter Who Quietly Got Rich

He wasn't a doctor. He wasn't a lawyer. He didn't run a business or work on Wall Street. He was a waiter.

He worked long shifts at a small restaurant, lived in a modest apartment, and didn't spend more than he earned. His friends assumed he didn't have much.

But what they didn't know was that he had been investing since his early twenties. Not a lot - just a little from every paycheck. No flashy stocks, no get - rich - quick moves. Just consistency.

By the time he was in his 50s, his quiet strategy had paid off. He had built a seven - figure investment portfolio - without ever making a six - figure income.

What He Knew (That Most People Don't)

Money doesn't have to be complicated. But if no one ever explained it to you, it *feels* like it is.

Here's the truth:
You don't need a finance degree.
You don't need a big paycheck.
You don't even need to get everything right.

What you do need is:

- **Time**
- **Consistency**
- **A willingness to be different from everyone else**

What Most People Do (And Why It Backfires)

Most people try to *look* successful instead of *building* success. They spend their money as fast as it comes in - on things that lose value the second they're bought. They avoid investing because it sounds confusing. Or they wait until they "make more money." But waiting is the most expensive mistake you can make.

The Power of Starting Early

Here's a visual that explains it better than any words can:

Visual: *The Power of Time*

Person	Invests	Years Contributed	Stops at Age	Total at 60 (7% return)
A (Early Start)	$100/month	Age 18–28 (11 years)	28	~$168,500
B (Late Start)	$100/month	Age 30–60 (31 years)	60	~$122,700

Even though Person A only invested for **11 years**, they ended up with **more** than Person B who invested for **three times as long** - because they started earlier and let their money grow.

What This Means for You

- You don't have to invest a ton.
- You don't have to be rich.
- You don't have to time the market.

You just have to *start* - and give your money time to grow.

Let's Keep It Simple

This book isn't going to flood you with financial jargon or unrealistic expectations. It's not about becoming a millionaire overnight. It's about learning how money really works - so you can avoid the traps most people fall into. You don't need to be perfect. You just need to be consistent.

Let's get started.

Chapter 2: The Power of Starting Early

The Earlier You Plant, the Bigger Your Tree Grows

A Tale of Two Friends

At 18, both Ilene and Luis got part - time jobs. Ilene started setting aside just $100 a month into a basic investment account. **Luis** said, **"I'll wait until I'm making more."**

Ilene stopped investing by age 28 - just 10 years in. Luis finally started at 30 and invested the same $100 a month until age 60. Guess who had more money by the time they retired?

It wasn't Luis.

The Power of Compound Growth

This is called **compound growth**. It's when:

- Your money earns money (interest)
- Then *that* money earns more money
- Over time, the growth gets faster and bigger

The earlier you start, the more time you give that snowball to roll.

"Compound interest is the most powerful force in the universe."
(Albert Einstein may or may not have said this, but it's still true.)

The Math Behind It

Person	Start Age	Stop Age	Years Invested	Total Invested	Value at 60 (7% return)
Ilene	18	28	11	$13,200	~$168,500
Luis	30	60	31	$37,200	~$122,700

Even though Ilene only invested for 11 years, she ended up with more money than Luis - because they started early and gave compound growth time to work.

Why Most People Don't Do This

- They think $100/month is "too small to matter"
- They think they have time to catch up later
- They want to spend now and save "later"

But here's the truth:

If you wait, you'll spend the rest of your life playing catch - up.

What If You Start Later? Is It Too Late?

No.

Later is still better than never. And consistency still beats guessing.

But if you're reading this now and you *can* start early - even with $20, $50, or $100/month - do it. Let time work for you, not against you.

Simple Action Steps

- Open a Roth IRA or investment account (see Chapter 3 for how)
- Automate $25–$100/month if possible
- Don't panic if it goes up or down
- Stay consistent

Final Thought

The difference between *building wealth* and *struggling* with money isn't luck. It's whether you put time on your side to grow your money - or let time work against you through debt and bad decisions.

Chapter 3: Investing Without the Hype

Why the Boring Stuff Builds Real Wealth

Investing Isn't Just for Rich People

Most people think investing is something you do *after* you get rich.

But the truth is:
You invest to get rich.

You don't need a finance degree.
You don't need to "pick stocks."
You don't need to check the market every day.

You just need a simple strategy - and the discipline to stick with it.

Why Most People Are Intimidated

- The stock market sounds confusing
- The news makes it sound risky
- Social media pushes "hot tips" and quick wins

But those who *really* build wealth? They usually don't say much. They invest in simple things, hold them for decades, and don't panic.

Why Stashing Money Loses Value

Saving cash at home or in a safe deposit box might feel secure - but money loses its **purchasing power** every year because of inflation.

Year	Value of $100 if stashed	Purchasing Power (in today's $)
Now	$100	$100
5 years	$100	$86
10 years	$100	$74
20 years	$100	$55

Keeping **some emergency cash** is smart. But if your goal is to **grow wealth**, put your money in places where it can **work for you** (index funds, Roth IRA, etc.), instead of letting it shrink over time.

The Basics: What Are You Actually Investing In?

When you invest in stocks, you're buying pieces of companies. When those companies grow, your money grows.

There are **three common ways** to invest in the stock market:

Investment Type	What It Is	Pros	Cons
Individual Stocks	One specific company (like Apple or Tesla).	High potential reward	High risk, not diversified
Mutual Funds	A mix of many companies picked by a fund manager	Professional oversight	May charge higher fees
Index Funds/ETFs	A group of companies that track a whole market (like the S&P 500, top 500 companies in the U.S.)	Low cost, easy, diversified	Less exciting, slower short - term gains

For most people, especially beginners, **index funds and ETFs are the smartest choice**.

Why Index Funds Work So Well

An index fund spreads your money across hundreds (or thousands) of companies. If a few go down, others go up - and your money keeps growing over time. It's like betting on the whole league instead of one player.

Some great examples:

- **VTSAX/VTI** - Vanguard Total U.S. stock market
- **VFIAX/VOO** - Vanguard S&P 500
- **FXAIX** - Fidelity's low - cost S&P 500
- **SWPPX/SCHX** - Schwab S&P 500

How to Actually Start

You can open an account with:

- **Vanguard** – popular for long - term investors. Many of their index funds require a **$3,000 minimum initial investment** (a one - time buy - in). After that, you can add as much or as little as you want. Their ETFs have **no minimum** (you can start with the price of one share).

- **Fidelity** – very beginner - friendly. **No minimums** on most index funds, and you can even buy **fractional shares** (great for starting with $5 or $10).

- **Charles Schwab** – also **no minimums** for their index funds and ETFs, making it easy to start small.

Note: You don't have to use these three. There are many financial institutions and apps out there. Just be cautious with third - party investment platforms - sometimes they charge **higher expense ratios** (hidden fees) that quietly eat away at your returns over time.

Expense Ratio (ER) – Explained Simply
An expense ratio is just the **fee** you pay every year for a fund to manage your money.

- If a fund has an expense ratio of **0.05%**, that means you pay **5 cents for every $100** you invest.
- If it's **1%**, that's **$1 for every $100**.

It doesn't sound like much, but over decades, high fees can eat away **tens of thousands of dollars** from your investments.

That's why low - cost index funds are so powerful - their expense ratios are usually **close to zero**, while some third - party funds or actively managed funds charge much more.

You'll need to choose an account type:

Account Type	Good For	Tax Benefits	Notes
Roth IRA	Retirement	Grows tax - free	Best if you're under income limits
Traditional IRA	Retirement	Tax - deductible taxed later	May lower your taxable income today

Account Type	Good For	Tax Benefits	Notes
Brokerage Account	Flexible investing	Taxed on gains	No limits on contributions or Withdrawals

What About Crypto, Meme Stocks, or Day Trading?

You'll hear a lot of hype. And yes - some people *do* make money with these.

But most people don't.

They:

- Buy high when everyone's talking about it
- Panic sell when it drops
- End up broke or burned out

If you want to take a small amount of "play money" and experiment? That's fine. But build your *real* wealth with proven strategies first.

Think of hype investing like hot sauce - it's okay in small doses, but it can ruin the whole meal if you overdo it.

Common Myths (and the Truth)

Myth	Reality
"I need a lot of money to invest"	You can start with $1 or $5
"I'll lose it all in a crash"	Only if you panic and sell
"It's too late for me"	Later is still better than never
"I need to pick the best stocks"	Index funds already include top companies

Action Steps

- Choose a platform (Fidelity, Vanguard, Schwab)
- Open a **Roth IRA** or **brokerage account**
- Set up automatic monthly investments into a **low - cost index fund**
- Leave it alone and let it grow

Special Note for Military Members

If You're in the Military - Use the TSP

If you're serving in the military under the Blended Retirement System (BRS), you have access to the **Thrift Savings Plan (TSP)** - one of the best retirement tools in the country.

Here's how it works:

- **You can contribute from Day 1** - even 10%, 15%, or more of your base pay.
- The government adds **1% automatically** after 60 days.
- After **two years of service**, they start matching up to **4%** of your contributions. That's free money.
- At the two - year mark, you're **vested** - meaning you keep the government's contributions even if you leave the service.

Pro tip: Set up at least 5% from your very first paycheck so you're already ready for the match when it kicks in.

Picking Investments in the TSP

Inside your TSP, you get to choose where your money goes. The funds range from safe to risky:

Individual Funds

- **G Fund** - Safest. No risk to your original investment. Low returns.
- **F Fund** - Bonds. Low - medium risk.
- **C Fund** - Large U.S. companies (S&P 500). Solid growth, medium risk.
- **S Fund** - Small/mid - sized U.S. companies. Higher growth, higher risk.
- **I Fund** - International stocks. Higher risk, global exposure.

Lifecycle (L) Funds

- Pre - mixed portfolios based on your target retirement date.
- Young = more aggressive (more C, S, I funds).
- Older = more conservative (more G and F funds).
- Example: **L 2065** starts aggressive today, becomes safer over time.

Avoid the Common Traps

Too many service members (and young adults in general) blow deployment pay or bonuses on:

- Overpriced cars with sky - high interest rates
- Rent - to - own furniture
- Electronics and "fun" purchases that lose value immediately

These traps keep you broke and make someone else rich. Instead, pay yourself first - contribute to your TSP or other investments before spending on wants.

Keep It Simple

- If you're young, lean toward growth funds (C, S, I or an aggressive L Fund).
- If you're closer to needing the money, move toward safer funds (G, F, conservative L Funds).
- Don't try to time the market. Pick a plan, stick with it, and let it grow.

Special Note for Public Service Jobs - Deferred Compensation (457b)

If you work for a county, city, or state - police, fire, EMT, or other public service - you may have access to a **457(b) Deferred Compensation Plan**.

It works a lot like a 401(k), but with extra flexibility:

- **Traditional 457(b):** Contributions come out before taxes, lowering your taxable income today. You'll pay taxes when you withdraw.
- **Roth 457(b):** Contributions are after - tax, but withdrawals are tax - free later.

Big advantage: If you leave your job, you can take money out without the 10% early withdrawal penalty most retirement accounts charge.

Don't skip this just because "retirement is far away." Even small amounts now can grow into serious money later.

Bottom Line:
Whether you're in the military or not, the rules are the same - start early, contribute consistently, and don't get distracted by hype or "hot tips." The earlier you plant the seed, the bigger the tree grows.

Final Thought

Wealth doesn't come from doing something exciting - it comes from doing something smart, over and over again.

Boring investing works.
It's slow at first.
Then it snowballs.
Stay patient.

Here's a **High - Interest Car Loan Cost** graph showing how much more you pay over time for a $40K car at 12% APR over 6 years.

This visual will hit home for young adults - especially those tempted to spend like they're already wealthy - by showing how interest piles up and can easily add thousands to the price of a car.

Total Cost of a High-Interest Car Loan
($40,000 at 12% APR for 6 years)

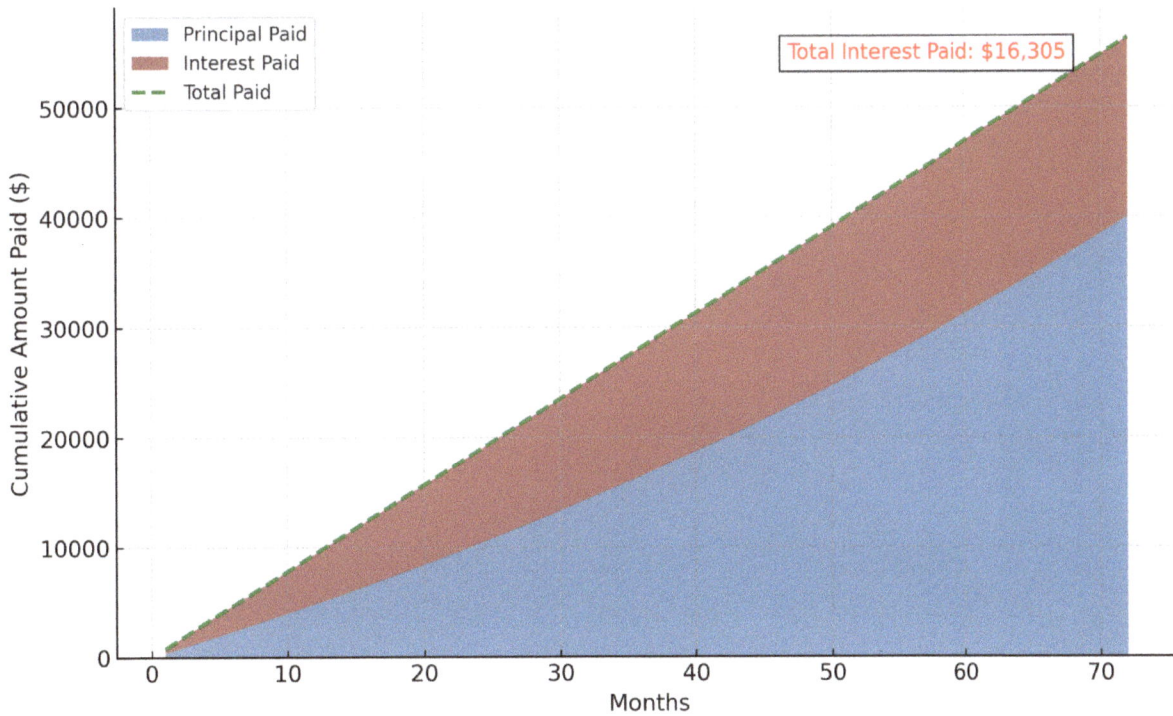

Legend:
- Principal Paid
- Interest Paid
- Total Paid

Total Interest Paid: $16,305

X-axis: Months
Y-axis: Cumulative Amount Paid ($)

Here's a **Credit Card Interest Cost** graph for a $2,000 balance at 24% APR with only $50/month minimum payments.

This clearly shows how high - interest credit card debt drags on for years and racks up massive interest over time and it is a perfect visual for warning young adults.

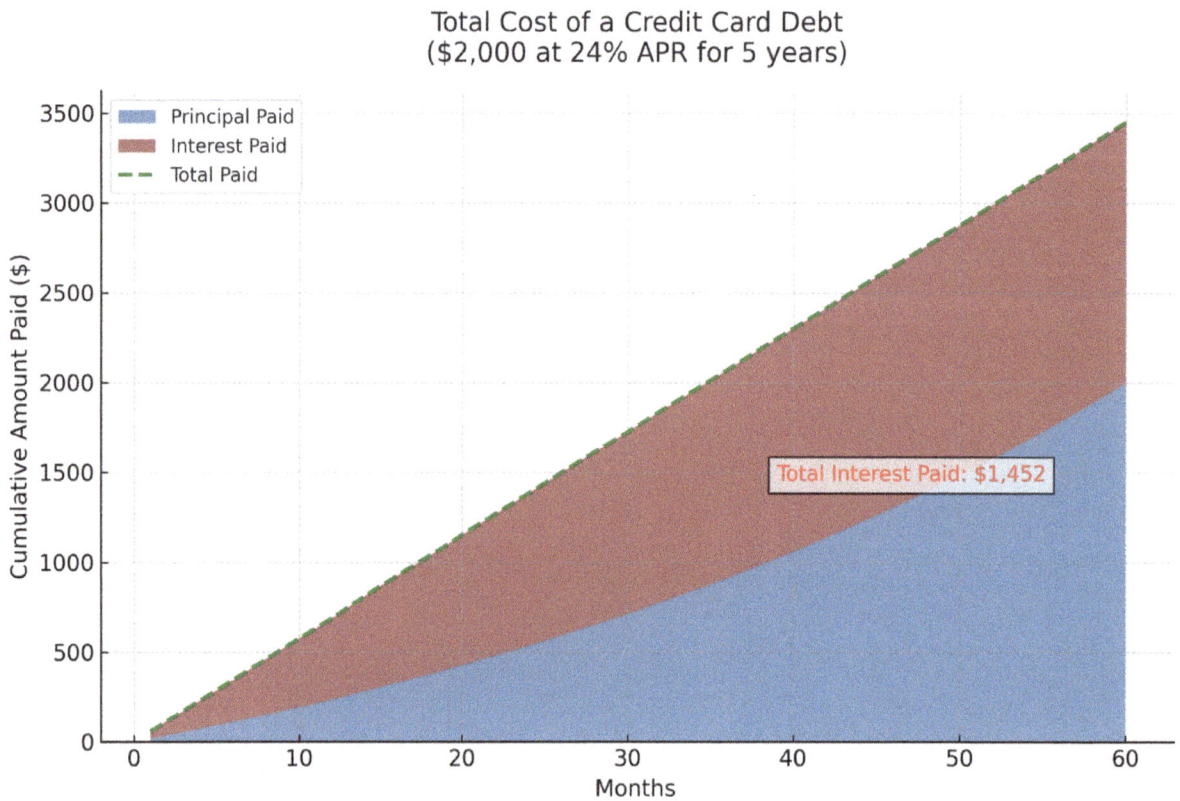

Total Cost of a Credit Card Debt
($2,000 at 24% APR for 5 years)

Legend:
- Principal Paid
- Interest Paid
- Total Paid

Total Interest Paid: $1,452

Y-axis: Cumulative Amount Paid ($) — 0, 500, 1000, 1500, 2000, 2500, 3000, 3500

X-axis: Months — 0, 10, 20, 30, 40, 50, 60

Chapter 4: Taxes and Capital Gains

What You Don't Know Will Cost You

Why You Can't Ignore Taxes

You work hard. You save. You invest. But when it's time to take some money out - you realize there's a new player at the table: **the IRS**.

Taxes aren't just something your parents worry about. If you earn money, invest, or plan to build wealth - you *have* to understand the basics.

The 3 Big Tax Categories You Should Know

Tax Type	What It Covers	When It Affects You
Income Tax	Money you earn from working (job, freelance, etc.)	Every paycheck or self - employed income
Capital Gains Tax	Profit from selling investments or assets	When you sell stocks, crypto, real estate, etc.
Sales/Other Taxes	Everyday purchases, property, vehicles, etc.	All the time (gas, groceries, cars, etc.)

Capital Gains: The One That Sneaks Up on People

Capital gains are the profits you make when you sell something for more than you paid.

Examples:

- You buy a stock at $100, sell it at $150 → **$50 gain**
- You invest in crypto at $5,000, sell at $8,000 → **$3,000 gain**
- You sell a house for $50K more than you bought it → **Capital gain**

Seems great, right?
Well... here comes the tax part.

Short - Term vs. Long - Term Capital Gains

Type of Gain	How Long You Held It	Tax Rate
Short - Term	1 year or less	Taxed like your income (10%–37%)
Long - Term	More than 1 year	Lower rate (0%, 15%, or 20%)

Key takeaway: If you hold investments *at least one year*, you'll usually pay less in taxes.

Real - World Example:

You make $40,000 a year and sell a stock for a **$1,000 gain**:

- If you held it for 3 months → it's short - term → taxed at your normal income tax rate (likely 12% or more)
- If you held it for 13 months → it's long - term → taxed at a lower rate (could be 0%)

That's a big difference - for doing nothing more than waiting.

What About When You Sell a House?

If you sell your home and make a profit, **you can avoid taxes on up to:**

- **$250,000** in profit (if single)
- **$500,000** in profit (if married filing jointly)

BUT ONLY IF:

- You lived in the house for 2 out of the last 5 years
- It was your primary residence

If you flip homes, rent them out, or sell them quickly, different rules apply.

What About Crypto?

Yes - **crypto is taxed**.
If you sell Bitcoin, Ethereum, or NFTs for a profit - it's a capital gain. If you use crypto to *buy something* (like a car or food), and the crypto went up in value before you spent it, that's also a taxable event.

Dividends and Interest: Yep, That's Taxed Too

If you earn money from:

- **Dividends** (companies paying you for holding stock)
- **Interest** (from savings accounts or bonds)

That money usually gets taxed in the year you receive it. It might not be much at first - but it adds up.

How to Prepare (Without Going Crazy)

- **Track what you sell** - Your brokerage will send you tax forms each year
- **Keep your records** - Know when you bought something and how much you paid
- **Use tools** like TurboTax, FreeTaxUSA, or a local tax preparer
- **Don't panic** - You only pay taxes when you actually sell or withdraw

Pro Tips

- Want to sell some stocks but avoid taxes? Consider selling after the one - year mark
- Want to lower your tax bill? Hold your investments longer
- Have investments that lost value? You may be able to use those losses to *reduce* your tax bill

Quick Note on When Taxes Show Up

When you sell investments like stocks or mutual funds, or if you take money out of certain retirement accounts, you won't get a tax bill right away. Instead, you'll usually pay those taxes the following year when you file. And if you pull money from a retirement account before age 59½, you might also face a 10% penalty on top of taxes. The key takeaway: be mindful of when you cash out, because those choices today could surprise you at tax season.

Final Thought

Taxes aren't fun - but they're part of the game. And once you understand the rules, it's a lot easier to win.

Chapter 5: Credit Cards That Work *For* You

(Not Against You)

Build Credit, Earn Rewards, and Stay in Control

Why Credit Cards Scare People

Let's be real - credit cards have a bad reputation.
And it's not undeserved. A lot of people:

- Swipe without a plan
- Carry balances they can't pay off
- Get buried in debt, fees, and regret

But the problem isn't the card. It's how you use it.

Used the wrong way, credit cards are traps.
Used the right way, they're *tools* - to build credit, earn rewards, and save money.

Credit Card Myths vs. Reality

Myth	Truth
Credit cards are evil	They're neutral - it depends how you use them
You need to carry a balance to build credit	False. Pay in full each month to build credit *and* avoid interest
Debit cards are safer	Credit cards offer better fraud protection
Rewards cards are a scam	They're not - *if* you don't pay interest

---

How Credit Cards Actually Work

- You borrow money from the bank
- You agree to pay it back every month
- If you pay it all off by the **due date**, you owe **zero** interest
- If you don't? You'll be charged interest - often **20% or more**

Think of it as a short - term loan that's only free *if* you're disciplined

---

What Credit Card Companies Hope You Don't Do:

- Read the fine print
- Pay attention to interest rates (APR)
- Pay your full balance on time

Because when you don't - they make money off of *you*. But when you're smart? You use *them* instead.

Why Credit Cards Matter for Young Adults

1. **Build Your Credit Score**
   - A higher score = better rates on cars, apartments, and mortgages
   - Your score is like a trust rating - the higher it is, the more opportunities you get
2. **Start Earning Rewards**
   - Cash back, points for flights, hotel stays, or even rent
   - You can earn *while spending the same amount* - if you pay it off monthly
3. **Learn Financial Discipline Early**
   - Credit cards can *teach* responsibility - when used with boundaries

---

How to Use a Credit Card the *Right* Way

- Only spend what you can pay off every month
- Set auto - pay to pay your full balance
- Use it like a debit card - but smarter
- Track your spending weekly - not when the bill shows up
- Pick a rewards card that matches your lifestyle

Best Starter Cards to Consider

Card	Type	Perks	Notes
Discover It Student Cash Back	Beginner	5% rotating categories	Great for first - time users
Chase Freedom Unlimited	Cash back	1.5% on everything, no annual fee	Good long - term card (*Requires one to pair with Sapphire Preferred to use points for travel*)

Card	Type	Perks	Notes
BILT Mastercard	Points for rent	Earn points on rent without fees	Can transfer to travel partners
Apple Card	Cash back	2% via Apple Pay, visual spending tracker	Requires iPhone

Choose a card with **no annual fee** and a simple reward structure when starting out.

How Credit Card Rewards Work

Most cards earn:

- **Points** or **Cash back** (e.g. 1% = 1 point per $1)
- Some let you **transfer points** to airlines/hotels for big value
- Others give you **straight cash back** into your account

Example:
Spend $500/month on a 2% cash back card = $10/month in rewards
That's $120/year - just for using a smarter payment method.

What Is a Credit Score - and Why It Matters

Here's the breakdown of what goes into your score and how much "weight" each category carries:

Factor	Weight
Payment History	35%
Credit Utilization	30%
Length of Credit History	15%
Credit Mix	10%
New Credit	10%
Total	**100%**

Together these factors make up your entire credit score - 100%. Pay on time. Keep balances low. Let accounts age. That's the game.

What Not to Do

Don't carry a balance "to build credit"
Don't open a bunch of cards at once
Don't use a credit card to buy things you can't afford
Don't ignore due dates - set reminders or autopay

Quick Example of Smart Credit Use:

You get a credit card with a $1,000 limit. Each month, you spend $200 on things you already buy (groceries, gas). You pay it off in full by the due date. You never pay interest. You earn cash back. Your credit score grows.

That's how you win.

Final Thought

Credit cards can be a trap - or a tool. The choice is in how you use them.

Used wisely, they help you build credit, earn rewards, and take control of your financial future. Used poorly, they dig a hole.

Start smart. Stay in control.

Chapter 6: Side Hustles, LLCs, and Making Extra Money

How to Start Small, Earn More, and Build Something of Your Own

---

Beyond the 9 - to - 5

A steady job is important - it helps cover your bills and keeps life running smoothly. You might consider adding to your paycheck with starting a side hustle.

You might consider this if:

- You're working part - time or hourly
- You have student loans, rent, and car payments
- You want to save and invest on top of surviving

That's where **side income** comes in.

You don't need to start a big company.
You don't need investors.
You just need a skill, some effort, and a plan.

What Is a Side Hustle?

A side hustle is anything you do to earn money *outside* your main job.

Examples:

- Babysitting or dog walking
- Hair/ makeup services
- Selling crafts or clothes online (e.g. eBay, Facebook Marketplace or Etsy)
- Car detailing, pressure washing, trash can cleaning
- Tutoring or teaching a skill
- Creating content or editing videos

If you can solve a problem or save someone time - you can get paid.

Side Hustle vs. Small Business

Side Hustle	Things to Consider	Small Business
Flexible	Time Commitment	More structured
None or very simple	Legal Setup	Usually needs official setup
Extra money	Goal	Growth, systems, scaling
Report income	Taxes	May need business tax return

You don't need to start with a business plan. Start by offering value. Learn as you go.

Do I Need an LLC?

Not always.

LLC = *Limited Liability Company*
It separates *you* from your business, which can protect you legally.

You might want one if:

- You're working with clients
- You handle people's property
- You're making decent money ($5K+/year)
- You want to open a business bank account or credit card

But if you're just starting out? You can wait. Keep things simple.

Business Tools That Make Life Easier

- **Payment apps**: Venmo, Cash App, PayPal, Square
- **Invoicing**: Wave (free), QuickBooks (paid)
- **Website/booking tools**: Linktree, Calendly, Wix
- **Banking**: A separate checking account, even without an LLC, helps you stay organized
- **Business credit cards**: Once you're legit, you can start earning points or cashback *for your business expenses*

What About Taxes?

If you earn more than $400/year from your side hustle, the IRS considers it **self - employment**.

That means:

- You may owe **self - employment tax** (about 15%)
- You'll report income on a tax form called **Schedule C**
- You can **deduct expenses** (tools, supplies, gas, equipment, etc.)

Keep records of what you earn and spend. It doesn't have to be fancy - Google Sheets works fine.

Pros and Cons of Starting Your Own Hustle

Pros	Cons
Flexible hours	No guaranteed income
Unlimited potential	More responsibility
Can grow into something bigger	Must track taxes and expenses
Builds confidence and skills	Takes time and patience

The Mindset Shift

A side hustle isn't just about extra money.
It's about realizing **you can create value.**

You don't have to wait for someone to "give you" a raise.
You can go out and **earn more - on your terms.**

Final Thought

You already have what you need to get started: your time, your effort, and your ideas.

Start with one thing.
Solve one problem.
Earn your first $100.
Then scale from there.

Chapter 7: Budgeting That Doesn't Suck

Give Every Dollar a Job - And Still Have a Life

What Most People Think Budgeting Means

- No eating out
- No fun
- Just bills, bills, bills

But a **real budget** isn't about cutting everything out. It's about choosing where your money goes - *before* it disappears.

A budget isn't a cage. It's a plan for freedom.

Why You Need a Budget - Even If You're "Broke"

- To stop wondering where your money went
- To avoid overdraft fees or credit card debt
- To actually build savings, instead of wishing for it

Even if you're only working part - time or earning a little, **you can still budget**. And if you learn this skill now? You'll stay ahead for life.

The 50/30/20 Budget (Simple & Flexible)

Category	% of Income	What It Covers
Needs	50%	Rent, food, bills, transportation, insurance
Wants	30%	Dining out, clothes, hobbies, fun
Saving & Debt	20%	Emergency fund, investing, paying off credit cards or loans

This formula works whether you're earning $500/month or $5,000/month.

You can also tweak it to fit your lifestyle, for example:

- 70/20/10
- 60/30/10
- Or even 80/10/10 if you're in survival mode

Real - World Example: Monthly Income = $2,000

Category	Budgeted Amount	Notes
Needs (50%)	$1,000	Rent, groceries, phone, gas
Wants (30%)	$600	Fun, food out, subscription services
Saving/Debt (20%)	$400	$200 to Roth IRA, $100 emergency fund, $100 credit card payment

What Counts As a "Need" vs. a "Want"?

Item	Need/Want	Why
Groceries	Need	You have to eat
Streaming services	Want	Not essential
Car insurance	Need	Required to drive
New shoes (*just because*)	Want	You *want* them, but you don't *need* them
Emergency fund	Saving	Future - proofing your life

You don't have to give up everything you enjoy. You just need to stop spending on autopilot.

The Power of Tracking

You can't improve what you don't track.

Try this:

- For 30 days, write down **every dollar you spend**
- You'll be shocked where the leaks are
- Then adjust your spending with intention

Tools to help:

- **Mint** (free)
- **YNAB (You Need A Budget)** (paid, but powerful)
- **Good old pen and paper or Google Sheets**

Avoiding Lifestyle Creep

Lifestyle creep = when your income goes up… and so does your spending.

You earn more → you upgrade your car, your clothes, your food…
And suddenly you're still living paycheck to paycheck - just with nicer stuff.

Give yourself permission to upgrade slowly. Keep your budget grounded - even when your income grows.

Emergency Fund 101

Everyone needs one - even if it's just $500 to start.

It protects you from:

- Car repairs
- Job loss
- Medical bills
- Surprise expenses that would normally go on a credit card

Start small. Build up to 3–6 months of essential expenses over time.

Budgeting When You're in Debt

If you're in debt, part of your "savings" category should go to **paying it down**.
Start with:

- **Pay the minimum** on all your debts (so you don't fall behind).

- Take any **extra money** you have and choose one of these:

  - **Snowball Method:** Pay off the **smallest balance first** → gives you quick wins and momentum.
  - **Avalanche Method:** Pay off the **highest interest rate first** → saves you the most money long - term.

The faster you knock out debt, the more freedom you gain each month.

Example

- **Credit Card:** $10,000 at **22% interest** (highest rate, big balance).
- **Car Loan:** $7,000 at **8% interest** (medium rate, smaller balance).
- **Student Loan:** $20,000 at **5% interest** (lowest rate, largest balance).
- **Monthly Budget:** $1,000 (enough to pay minimums and a little extra).

Snowball Method

- Focused on the **smallest balance first** → the **car loan ($7K)**.
- That debt disappeared fastest, giving an **emotional win** (one whole bill gone).
- After that, extra money rolled into the credit card, then finally into the student loan.
- **Total payoff time:** about **60 months (5 years)**.

Avalanche Method

- Focused on the **highest interest rate first** → the **credit card (22%)**.
- It took longer to see the first debt disappear, but because the avalanche was killing off the most expensive debt early, interest charges dropped much faster.
- After the credit card was gone, money rolled into the car loan and then into the student loan.
- **Total payoff time:** about **53 months (just under 4½ years)**.

The Results

- **Snowball:** Motivating - one debt cleared quickly, but more interest was paid overall → longer total payoff (60 months).
- **Avalanche:** Less "feel - good" at first (big credit card balance takes time), but it **saved money** and shaved off **7 months** of payments (53 months total).

The Lesson

There's **no wrong answer**

- If you need motivation and quick wins → Snowball works best.
- If you want the fastest, cheapest way out of debt → Avalanche is the winner.

It really depends on your personality: do you need momentum, or do you want efficiency?

Final Thought

Budgeting isn't about being perfect. It's about being *in control*.

If you don't give your money a job - it'll disappear. Make a plan. Adjust when needed. Stay consistent.

Chapter 8: Buying a Car That Won't Break You

You Don't Need a Lambo. You Need to Get Where You're Going.

Let's Be Honest: Cars Are Expensive

They're one of the biggest purchases most young adults make early on.
And they *seem* like a symbol of freedom and success...

Until:

- The car note hits
- The insurance skyrockets
- You realize gas, maintenance, and repairs don't care how cool your rims are

---

What You Really Need

You don't need the flashiest car in the parking lot.
You need:

- Something reliable
- Something fuel - efficient
- Something that won't wreck your budget

A car should take you to your goals - not delay them.

New vs. Used: What's Smarter?

Option	Pros	Cons
New Car	Warranty, latest features, no wear and tear	Expensive, depreciates fast, higher insurance
Used Car	Cheaper, less depreciation, lower insurance	Might need repairs, less tech, shorter warranty

Rule of thumb:
Buy **used** if you're on a tight budget.
Buy **new** only if you can afford it *without* sacrificing your financial future.

Total Cost of Car Ownership

It's more than the sticker price.

Here's what you'll need to budget for:

Category	Estimated Monthly Cost
Car Payment	$250–$600+
Insurance	$100–$300+ (more if you're under 25)
Gas	$100–$250
Maintenance/Repairs	$50–$100 average
Registration/DMV Fees	Varies by state

Even a modest car can cost **$500–$1,000/month** when all is said and done.

How to Buy a Car the Smart Way

1. **Know your budget**
   Stick to a car that costs no more than 15–20% of your annual income
   (If you earn $30K/year, that's around $4,500–$6,000 total)
2. **Get pre - approved for a loan**
   It shows sellers you're serious and protects you from sketchy financing
3. **Check insurance rates before you buy**
   Sports cars, new models, and certain brands cost *way* more to insure
4. **Have a mechanic inspect any used car**
   Spend $100 now to avoid $2,000 in repairs later
5. **Avoid "buy here, pay here" car lots**
   They prey on people with bad credit and charge insane interest rates

Leasing vs. Buying

Option	Good For	Warning
Leasing	People who want a new car every 2–3 years	You don't own the car, and going over mileage costs you
Buying	People who want long - term value	Higher up - front cost, but better over time

If you're young and trying to save, **buying a used car outright or with a small loan is usually best**.

Car Loans: What to Watch For

- **Interest rate**: Based on your credit score. The lower the better.
- **Loan term**: Avoid going over 60 months (5 years). Longer = more interest.
- **Monthly payment**: Make sure it fits in your budget with everything else.
- **Total cost**: Focus on how much you'll pay **overall**, not just monthly.

If a car loan feels "affordable" only because it's stretched out over 6 or 7 years - it's too much car.

When to Say No

Don't buy a car if:

- You're already struggling with other debt
- You're only working part - time
- Your emergency fund is $0
- You're buying it just to impress people

Buy a car when:

- You have savings
- You've done the research
- You know the full cost, and you can afford it without wrecking your other goals

---

Final Thought

A car doesn't make you successful. Staying financially free does. Drive something you can afford. Invest the difference. And remember: the richest people don't always drive the flashiest cars.

Chapter 9: Renting vs. Owning a Home

When to Rent, When to Buy, and What No One Tells You

Owning a Home Is a Big Goal - But Is It Your Goal Right *Now*?

For many, buying a home feels like **"making it."** But it's also one of the biggest decisions - and expenses - you'll ever take on.

Before jumping in, you need to understand:

- What it actually costs
- When it's worth it
- And how it can either build wealth or create stress

Renting: Pros & Cons

Pros	Cons
Flexible - move anytime	Rent can go up each year
Fewer responsibilities	No equity or ownership
Landlord handles repairs	Rules on pets, paint, etc.
Good for short - term stays	You're helping *their* wealth grow

Renting makes sense if:

- You're not sure where you'll live long - term
- You're still saving for a down payment
- You want low responsibility

Buying: Pros & Cons

Pros	Cons
Builds equity over time	High upfront costs
You control the property	You're responsible for everything
Can lock in your monthly payment	Home values can drop
Potential for long - term wealth	Less flexibility to move

Buying makes sense if:

- You plan to stay in one place for 5+ years
- You have stable income and savings
- You understand the true costs

The Real Costs of Buying a Home

It's more than just your mortgage.

Cost	What to Expect
Down Payment	3.5% (FHA), 5%, or 20% to avoid PMI
Closing Costs	2%–5% of home price
PMI (Private Mortgage Insurance)	~$100–$300/month if under 20% down
Property Taxes	Varies by area - often $200–$600/month
Homeowners Insurance	~$100–$200/month
Maintenance & Repairs	Set aside 1% of home value per year
Furniture & Appliances	Can be thousands depending on size of home

Down Payment Example

You want to buy a $350,000 home:

Scenario	Down Payment	Monthly PMI?
3.5% (FHA)	$12,250	Yes
5%	$17,500	Yes
20%	$70,000	No

Avoiding PMI saves money - but it requires a much larger upfront investment.

Mortgage Terms: The Basics

- **Fixed - rate loan** = Same payment every month
- **Adjustable - rate (ARM)** = Can change over time (often risky)
- **30 - year loan** = Lower monthly payments
- **15 - year loan** = Higher payments, less interest over time

Choose fixed - rate unless you know exactly what you're doing.

Should I Buy With a Partner or Friend?

Think carefully.
If your name is on the loan, *you're responsible* - even if the other person stops paying.

Get everything in writing – legally, even with family.

Using Your Home as a Wealth Tool

Once you own a home and build up equity (the value of the home minus what you owe), you can access that value in a few ways:

1. **Home Equity Loan** - A lump sum with fixed interest
2. **HELOC** - A credit line based on your equity
3. **Cash - Out Refinance** - Replace your mortgage with a bigger one and take the difference in cash

These can be used for:

- Home upgrades
- Paying off high - interest debt
- Or **investing in another property** (which brings us to the next section...)

Extra Payments: Small Moves, Big Results

One of the simplest ways to save on your mortgage is to make **extra principal payments**.

- Even adding **$100/month** can shave years off your loan and save tens of thousands in interest.
- If you can afford more, that's even better. Think of it as giving yourself a guaranteed return - every extra dollar reduces future interest owed.
- You don't need a fancy strategy. Just add the extra payment toward "principal only" each month.

One thing to know: Paying off your mortgage faster means you'll lose out on some tax deductions for mortgage interest. But most people will find the money saved on interest (and the freedom of owning your home outright sooner) is worth much more than the small tax break they'd get from dragging out payments.

Here's the visual comparison for a **$250,000 loan at 6.5%**:

- **Normal Payments**:
  Loan term = **30 years (360 months)**
  Total interest paid ≈ **$317,281**
- **With +$100 Extra per Month**:
  Loan term = **25 years, 3 months (303 months)**
  Total interest paid ≈ **$259,092**

Savings: You pay off the loan almost **5 years sooner** and save about **$58,000 in interest**.

This chart clearly shows how the balance drops faster with the extra $100/month payment.

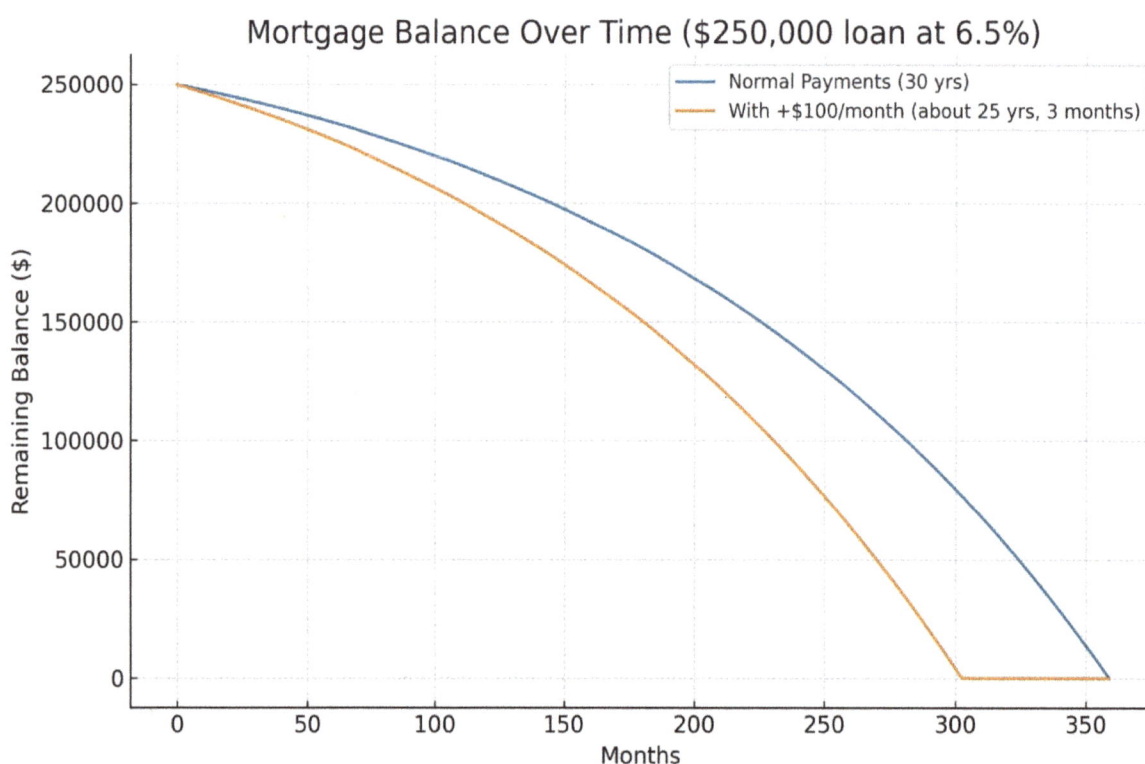

Mortgage Balance Over Time ($250,000 loan at 6.5%)

Bonus: How Real Estate Investors Avoid Taxes with a 1031 Exchange

Let's say you buy a small home, rent it out, and years later it's worth a lot more. If you sell it and make $100K in profit, that's a big **capital gains tax bill** coming your way.

Unless... you do a 1031 exchange.

What's a 1031 Exchange?

A **1031 exchange** lets you:

- Sell an investment property
- Use *all the profits* to buy another one
- And **delay paying capital gains taxes**

It's legal, powerful, and used by smart investors to build wealth faster.

Basic Rules

- Applies to **investment properties only** (not your home)
- You must **identify the new property** within 45 days
- You must **close** on it within 180 days
- You must **reinvest the full amount** (not just the profits)

Think of it like trading up - and pressing pause on the tax bill.

Why It Matters

If you keep reinvesting using 1031 exchanges, you can go from:

- A small condo → to a duplex → to an apartment building
- All without paying capital gains each time you "level up"

Eventually, if you pass those properties down to your kids, taxes can be forgiven entirely under current laws (*step - up in basis*). It means **your kids inherit the property at the current value, not what you originally paid, so the built - in capital gains tax essentially disappears.**

Passing Property to Your Kids (Step - Up in Basis)

Here's something most people don't know when you leave property to your kids, the IRS resets the property's value at today's market price. This is called a "step - up in basis."

Example:

- You bought a house years ago for $100,000.
- When you pass away, the house is worth $400,000.
- If your kids inherit it, their "new starting point" is $400,000.
- If they sell it right away for $400,000 → they owe no taxes.
- If they sell later for $420,000 → they only pay tax on the $20,000 gain, not the full $300,000.

This rule can save families a lot of money and is one reason real estate is such a powerful way to pass down wealth.

Important: Tax laws can change, so always check current rules with a professional.

Final Thought

Renting is temporary. Owning is responsibility. But both can be smart. The key is knowing what's right for your situation - and using real estate as a tool, not a trap.

Chapter 10: Understanding Assets & Liabilities

The Real Difference Between Building Wealth and Staying Broke

---

Why This Chapter Matters

Some people make $30,000 a year and get ahead. Others make $130,000 and still live paycheck to paycheck.

What's the difference?

Often, it comes down to this:
Assets vs. Liabilities

Simple Definitions

Term	What It Means	What It Does
Asset	Something you own that puts money in your pocket or grows in value	Builds wealth over time
Liability	Something you owe or own that takes money out of your pocket	Costs you money

---

Examples

Item	Asset or Liability?	Why
Savings account	Asset	Earns interest and builds security
Credit card balance	Liability	You owe money and pay interest
Rental property	Asset	Generates income (if rented profitably)
Personal car	Liability	Loses value, costs money every month
Student loans	Liability (for now)	You owe money - but could become an investment if it boosts earnings
Stock investments	Asset	Grows in value over time
Gaming console	Liability	Fun, but doesn't pay you back financially

The Trap: Thinking "Stuff" Makes You Rich

A nice car, expensive clothes, and name - brand everything *look* like wealth. But if they're draining your bank account, they're not assets - they're **liabilities**.

Meanwhile, someone investing quietly in index funds, driving a paid - off car, and living below their means is actually building real wealth.

Assets grow your money.
Liabilities shrink it.

Tandas / Cundinas (Rotating Savings)
Growing up, my family sometimes joined tandas (also called cundinas). Here's how they work:

- A group of people agree to put in a set amount of money every week or month.
- Each round, one person gets the whole pot.
- The cycle continues until everyone has had a turn.

It's a system built on **trust, discipline, and community support**. For some families, this method is a **lifesaver**. It can provide quick access to a lump sum for emergencies, bills, or important purchases - especially when banks aren't an option.

If tandas work for you and your community, that's great - they can be an excellent tool for discipline and support. **But if your main goal is to build wealth over time, investing in the stock market, index funds, or other assets will work much harder for you.**

Key Lesson: Tandas are great for saving discipline and community support - but they don't grow your money. If building wealth is the goal, look to assets that multiply over time.

How Net Worth Works

Net worth is the value of everything you own **minus** everything you owe.

Net Worth = Assets - Liabilities

Example:

- Assets:
    - $3,000 in savings
    - $5,000 in a Roth IRA

- o $2,000 car value
  - o Total: **$10,000**
- Liabilities:
  - o $4,000 in credit card debt
  - o $8,000 car loan
  - o Total: **$12,000**

Net Worth = $10,000 - $12,000 = –$2,000

You're not failing - you're just starting. The goal is to grow your assets while paying down your liabilities.

How to Shift the Balance in Your Favor

Spend less on things that lose value
Save for things that grow over time
Invest early - even if it's a little
Avoid debt that doesn't produce income
Buy tools, not toys

Asset - Building Mindset

Ask yourself before every major purchase:

Will this help me make money, save money, or grow my money?

If the answer is no - it's likely a liability.

Final Thought

The difference often isn't about being rich or broke - it's about knowledge. People who build wealth focus on buying assets that grow in value. People who struggle financially often end up buying things that only look like wealth but lose value quickly. Once you understand the difference, you can start shifting your money toward real assets and lasting growth.

Learn the difference.
Live by it.
And you'll always be ahead of the game.

Chapter 11: Money Moves for Young Parents

How to Build Wealth for Your Kids - Even If You're Still Figuring It Out

---

It's Not Too Early

If you're a parent - or planning to be - one of the best gifts you can give your kids isn't more toys or material things. It's a financial head start. Buying toys is fine but imagine if even a portion of that money went into a 529 account or other investment for their future.

That means:

- Teaching them early habits
- Setting up accounts in their name
- Creating opportunities, you never had

You don't need to be a financial expert.
You just need to care enough to start.

---

1. 529 Plan: For Future Education Costs

A **529 plan** is a tax - advantaged investment account for education.

What It's For	College, trade school, or some K–12 tuition
Tax Benefits	Grows tax - free, withdrawals are tax - free if used for qualified education
Contribution Limits	Varies by state - often $300K+ lifetime max
Who Controls It	You stay in control, even when the child becomes an adult
What If They Don't Go to College?	You can transfer it to another child or roll up to $35,000 into a Roth IRA (under new rules)

Even small monthly contributions add up. $25–$50/month starting when they're born can grow into thousands.

---

2. UTMA/UGMA Account: Flexible Investment for the Future

A **UTMA/UGMA** (custodial account) lets you invest in your child's name.

What It's For	Any purpose - education, car, first apartment, etc.
Tax Benefits	Some tax advantages, but not as strong as 529
Who Controls It	You manage it until your child turns 18–21 (depends on state)
Ownership	Once they reach the age of majority, it becomes 100% theirs

Unlike a 529, these funds can be used for anything - not just school. In my culture, it's common to celebrate milestones like a quinceañera or sweet 16. Accounts like these could be used to help with those expenses, or even toward a first car. The key is that the money is flexible - it's for your child's future, in whatever form that takes.

3. Roth IRA for Kids (Yes, It's a Thing)

If your child earns income - babysitting, lawn care, a part - time job, or even helping in your family business - they qualify to open a Custodial Roth IRA. You, as the parent or guardian, manage the account until they're an adult.

You can:

- Open the account in their name (with you as custodian)
- Fund it up to the amount they actually earned (up to $7,000/year limit)
- Let that money grow tax - free for decades

Even a child as young as 7 or 8 can qualify if the income is real, documented, and reported (for example, working in a parent's business). The earlier they start, the more time compounding has to work.

Key Note: Contributions can't be more than the child actually earned. If they made $2,000 mowing lawns, that's the max contribution for the year. *Earned income means money from actual work - not allowance or gifts.*

4. Start With What You Can

You don't need to max out accounts. Even small monthly investments add up when started early.

Amount/Month	Years	Avg Return (7%)	Total at 18
$25	18	7%	~$11,600
$50	18	7%	~$23,200
$100	18	7%	~$46,400

That's real opportunity for a car, school, business, or future home.

---

5. Teach Your Kids As You Go

You don't have to wait until *you* "have it all together."
Instead:

- Let them watch you save
- Talk about money at the dinner table
- Involve them in simple financial decisions ("Should we eat out or save that money for something bigger?")

Make money a **normal** topic - not a secret one.

Bonus Tip: Mommy/Daddy Match

Offer to "match" your child's savings, just like a 401(k).

Example:

- If your child saves $5 from birthday money, you match it with $5.
- This builds strong habits - and makes saving feel rewarding.

Final Thought

You don't need to be wealthy to raise financially smart kids. You just need to start early - and lead by example. Even if you're learning alongside them, you're giving them something powerful:

A better start than you had.

Chapter 12: Wills, Trusts, and Protecting What You're Building

It's Not Morbid - It's Mature.

Why This Chapter Is Here

You might be young.
You might be just starting to build wealth.
You might not have kids yet - or maybe you do.

But if something were to happen to you tomorrow…

- Who gets your stuff?
- Who takes care of your kids?
- Who makes decisions for you if you can't?

That's what this chapter is about: **protecting what you're working for.**

What Happens If You Don't Have a Plan?

If you pass away without a will:

- The **state decides who gets what**
- Your assets go through **probate** (a long, public, sometimes expensive process)
- If you have kids, the **court decides** who raises them

This isn't about fear. It's about taking responsibility - for yourself *and* your people.

What You Actually Need

You don't need a $1,000 lawyer right away.
Start with the basics. Here's what matters:

---

1. A Will

A legal document that says:

- Who gets your stuff
- Who becomes guardian of your kids
- Who's in charge of making sure your wishes are followed (executor)

You can write a simple will online using tools like:

- Trust & Will
- Fabric by Gerber Life
- Free Will
- Or even state - specific templates

Update your will when big life events happen (marriage, kids, home purchase, etc.)

---

2. A Trust (*Optional, But Powerful*)

A **trust** is like a will - but with more control and privacy.

- Helps avoid probate entirely
- Can hold property, bank accounts, life insurance
- Lets you set conditions like:

> "My child gets this money at 25, not 18"
> "This money can only be used for school or housing"

Trusts make sense if:

- You own a home or rental property
- You have kids
- You want to protect your assets long - term

---

3. Healthcare Directive & Power of Attorney

These documents let someone you trust:

- Make medical decisions **if you can't**
- Handle your financial matters (like paying bills) during emergencies

This is important for *everyone* - not just older people.

4. Name Your Beneficiaries

For things like:

- Life insurance
- Retirement accounts (401(k), Roth IRA)
- Bank accounts (you can add a "payable on death" designee)

Why it matters:
If you don't list a beneficiary, those accounts may go to probate - even if you have a will.

---

5. Life Insurance: If You Have Kids or Dependents

Term life insurance is affordable and provides peace of mind.

Example:

- $250,000–$500,000 of coverage
- For 20–30 years
- Costs ~$20–$40/month (if you're young and healthy)

Choose term (not whole life).
It's for protection - not investing.

Quick Checklist: Protect Your Stuff

Will
Beneficiaries on all accounts
Healthcare directive
Durable power of attorney
Life insurance (if you have kids or dependents)

Final Thought

It's not about planning for death. It's about protecting life - for the people you love. Taking care of this now doesn't make you weird, cold, or paranoid. It makes you a responsible adult. And if you've made it this far in this book? That's exactly what you are.

Chapter 13: How to Think About Money

So, You Don't Go Broke Trying to Look Rich

What Most People Get Wrong

Some of the people who **look** rich... aren't.

They have:

- High monthly payments
- No savings
- Credit card debt
- And no real plan

They've traded *appearance* for *freedom*.

Meanwhile, many people who actually **are** wealthy:

- Drive regular cars
- Wear normal clothes
- Don't post about it
- Have money quietly working in the background

Looking rich is loud.
Being wealthy is quiet.

The Trap of Lifestyle Creep

Lifestyle creep is when your income goes up... and so does your spending.

You start making more, so you:

- Move into a bigger apartment
- Buy a newer car
- Eat out more
- Upgrade your phone, your shoes, your habits

But even with a higher income, you feel just as broke. Because the money's always going out just as fast as it comes in.

Why Wealthy Thinking Is Different

People who build wealth think differently:

Spending Mindset	Wealth Mindset
"I want it now"	"Can I wait and grow this money?"
"How much is the monthly payment?"	"What's the total cost?"
"I deserve this"	"Future me deserves more freedom"
"I can always finance it"	"I'll save and buy it smart"

A Few Real Truths About Money

- You don't have to impress people who don't pay your bills
- People forget what you wore - but you live with your financial choices every day
- Your bank account is more important than your image
- Every dollar is a decision - either it grows your future or feeds your ego

It's Okay to Want Nice Things

This isn't about being cheap or never spending.

It's about:

- Spending with purpose
- Being patient
- Making sure your money *works for you* - not just disappears for show

You can absolutely:

- Take vacations
- Drive a nice car
- Live in a beautiful place

But do it in the right order.
Build the foundation *first*, then enjoy the rewards *later* - with peace of mind.

Signs You're Thinking the Right Way

You know your budget
You're investing consistently
You save before you spend
You say "no" sometimes - even when you can afford it
You're not worried about impressing anyone

Final Thought

Don't go broke trying to look rich.
Go quiet while you build.
Go big when you're free.

Chapter 14: You Don't Need to Be Rich to Start

You Just Need to Start

By now, you've learned a lot.

You know how money really works.
You know the difference between looking rich and building wealth.
You know that every decision - every dollar - can move you forward or hold you back.

And more importantly, you know that you don't need to be perfect. You just need to be intentional.

Let's be real:

- You won't always stick to your budget
- You might miss a payment or buy something dumb
- You'll make money mistakes - it's part of learning

But now you've got the tools to recover, reset, and keep going.

That's the difference.

You Don't Need to...

Be a financial expert
Start with a huge paycheck
Time the market
Impress anyone

You *Do* Need to...

Start small
Be consistent
Stay curious
Think long - term
Focus on what actually matters

Whether you're earning $200/week or $2,000/week - what you do with that money is what matters most.

And now you know how to use it *on purpose.*

Your first $1,000 saved matters more than your first "big purchase."
Your first investment matters more than your first brand - name item.
Your future is built in small, boring, powerful decisions - made now.

So, take action.
Open that account.
Start tracking your spending.
Read your next book.
Teach someone else what you just learned.

Your path is just beginning.

Final Thought

Keep it simple.
Keep it growing.
You've got this.

Chapter 15: Financial Terms You Can't Afford to Skip

Clear Definitions. Real - Life Examples. No Eye Rolls.

Why This Chapter Matters

You're not supposed to know all this. Most schools never taught it. But the world expects you to understand it anyway.

So, here's a cheat code:
These are the terms that come up over and over - on contracts, in conversations, in the fine print.

Knowing what they mean = making better decisions.
Skipping this stuff = paying for it later.

Banking & Budgeting

Term	What It Means	Why It Matters
Checking Account	Where your money lives for daily spending	Used for bills, groceries, rent, etc.
Savings Account	Holds money you don't plan to touch right away	Good for emergency funds or short - term goals
Overdraft	When you spend more than you have in checking	Often triggers fees - avoid if possible
Direct Deposit	Paycheck sent straight to your account	Faster and safer than paper checks
Auto - Pay	Bills paid automatically on due date	Helps avoid late fees - but make sure you have enough money in your account

Credit & Debt

Term	What It Means	Why It Matters
Credit Score	3 - digit number (300–850) showing how reliable you are with debt	Affects loans, interest rates, even housing
APR (Annual Percentage Rate)	Cost to borrow money, shown as a yearly interest rate	Lower = better. Watch this on credit cards
Minimum Payment	Smallest amount due on a credit card	Pay more than this or you'll fall into debt
Principal	The original amount borrowed	You pay this back, plus interest
Interest	The fee charged for borrowing money	Adds up fast if you don't pay off debt

Investing & Wealth Building

Term	What It Means	Why It Matters
Stock	A piece of ownership in a company	Stocks grow your money over time
Bond	A loan to a company or government that pays you back with interest	Lower risk, but lower returns
Index Fund	A group of many stocks bundled together	Safer and easier than picking individual stocks
ETF	A type of index fund you can trade like a stock	Good for beginners
Dividend	A payout some companies give to shareholders	Free money - but not guaranteed
Brokerage Account	Where you buy/sell investments	Needed to start investing outside retirement accounts
Roth IRA	A retirement account that grows tax - free	Best if you're young and in a lower tax bracket

Income, Taxes & Paychecks

Term	What It Means	Why It Matters
Gross Income	Your total pay before taxes	What your job *offers* you
Net Income	What you actually take home	What you *spend and budget* with
Withholding	The taxes your employer takes out of your paycheck	Helps cover your income taxes during the year
W - 2	Tax form from your employer	Used to file your taxes
1099	Tax form for freelancers or side hustlers	You pay your own taxes on this income

Home & Rent Terms

Term	What It Means	Why It Matters
Lease	A rental contract (usually 6 –12 months)	Read carefully - breaking it costs money
Security Deposit	Money you pay upfront in case of damage	Get it back if you treat the place right
PMI	Extra insurance added to mortgages under 20% down	Adds to monthly payment
Escrow	A third party that holds funds safely during a sale	Used during home buying to protect Both sides
Property Tax	Annual tax based on your home's value	Often included in your mortgage payment

Legal & Protection Terms

Term	What It Means	Why It Matters
Will	Legal doc that says who gets your stuff when you die	Avoids family confusion and court fights
Trust	Holds your assets and gives you more control than a will	Protects your legacy, avoids probate
Power of Attorney	Someone who can act on your behalf legally or financially	Crucial if you're ever injured or incapacitated
Beneficiary	The person who receives your money/ assets when you die	Name them on life insurance, bank accounts, etc.
Deductible	What you pay out of pocket before insurance kicks in	Higher deductible = lower monthly cost (usually)

Final Thought

Knowing these terms doesn't make you boring - it makes you *powerful*. Money doesn't speak a secret language. It just sounds complicated until someone breaks it down. Now you know the words - and how to use them.

Final Thoughts

I grew up in East Oakland, California. I went to public schools where we weren't taught about money, investing, or building wealth. Our parents did the best they could, but most of them didn't have this knowledge either. That's why I wrote this book - to give you the tools I wish I had when I was younger.

Don't play the victim. Don't wait for perfect conditions. Just start. This book may not cover everything, and some topics here are just the basics - that's your cue to keep learning. Pull out your phone, do your own research, and dig deeper.

Stop complaining about what others have if you're not willing to grow yourself. The tools are out there reading, audiobooks, podcasts, videos - all at your fingertips. Use them.

And when you're ready to make the bigger moves, consult a financial expert who can guide you through the more complex, high - impact strategies.

I'll be honest - even at my age, I don't know everything. There's still so much more I want to learn. But I do know this: The sooner you start, the sooner your future self will thank you.

Appendix I: Resources & Tools for Your Money Journey

📊 Calculators & Tools

- **Compound Interest Calculator (Investor.gov)**
  Website: www.investor.gov/financial - tools - calculators/calculators/compound - interest - calculator
- **Compound Interest Calculator (Bankrate)**
  Website: www.bankrate.com/calculators/savings/compound - interest - calculator - tool.aspx
- **Karl's Mortgage Calculator (App)** Available on iOS App Store and Google Play - search: "Karl's Mortgage Calculator"
- **Undebt.it - Debt Payoff Planner**
  Website: www.undebt.it

📚 Recommended Books

- *The Simple Path to Wealth* - JL Collins
- *The Richest Man in Babylon* - George S. Clason
- *The Psychology of Money* - Morgan Housel
- *Rich Dad Poor Dad* - Robert Kiyosaki
- *Choose Your Enemies Wisely* - Patrick Bet - David (perfect for those who love to hustle and want an entrepreneurial edge)

🎓 Free Financial Literacy Courses

- **Khan Academy - Financial Literacy (sponsored by Capital One)**
  Website: www.khanacademy.org/college - careers - more/financial - literacy
- **Capital One - Money & Life Program**
  Website: www.capitalone.com/financial - education/money - and - life

🌐 Websites to Keep Learning

- **Bogleheads (Low - Cost Investing Community)**
  Website: www.bogleheads.org
- **ChooseFI (Financial Independence Blog & Podcast)**
  Website: www.choosefi.com
- **Morningstar (Fund & ETF Research)**
  Website: www.morningstar.com

📱 Social Media Voices Worth Following

- **@mattthemoneyguy** (Instagram & TikTok) - beginner - friendly tips on budgeting, investing, and building wealth

- **@budgetdog** (Instagram, TikTok, YouTube) - practical budgeting systems and debt payoff strategies
- **@teach.kids.money** (Instagram & TikTok) - advice for parents teaching kids and teens about money
- **@cofield_advisor** (Instagram, YouTube, TikTok) - CPA and tax expert who makes complex money and tax strategies simple, helping people build businesses and generational wealth
- **@AviTravelz** (Instagram) - Tips on using credit card points to travel smarter, plus practical travel hacks. Also features a beginner - friendly course on the basics of earning and redeeming credit card points for trips.

⚠ Note: Social media is great for daily learning, but always double - check advice, compare sources, and consult professionals for major decisions.

Final Word

These tools and resources are here to get you started - but remember, the most important step is to **take action**. Test calculators, read books, try apps, and keep building.

www.ingramcontent.com/pod-product-compliance
Lightning Source LLC
Chambersburg PA
CBHW040146200326
41519CB00035B/7608